The Little Book of

FLOWERS

**BUSHEL
& PECK
BOOKS**

Published by Bushel & Peck Books, www.bushelandpeckbooks.com.

Bushel & Peck Books is dedicated to fighting illiteracy all over the world.
For every book we sell, we donate one to a child in need——book for book.
To nominate a school or organization to receive free books,
please visit www.bushelandpeckbooks.com.

Type set in Temeraire, Avenir Next, and Bebas.

Illustrations sourced from the Biodiversity Heritage Library and The Graphics Fairy. Other
image credits as follows: vine pattern: Nespola Designs/Shutterstock.com; graph paper
background: Vector Image Plus/Shutterstock.com. Taxonomy sourced from Wikipedia.

ISBN: 9781638191551

First Edition

Printed in the United States

10 9 8 7 6 5 4 3 2 1

The Little Book of
FLOWERS

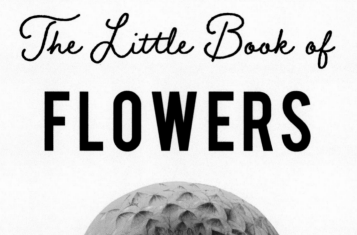

CHRISTIN FARLEY

Contents

1. SUNFLOWER 7

2. IRIS 9

3. MILKWEED 11

4. HYDRANGEA 13

5. TRILLIUM 15

6. BLACK-EYED SUSAN 17

7. CALIFORNIA POPPY 19

8. WOODLAND PHLOX 21

9. BLANKET FLOWER 23

10. CONEFLOWER 25

11. RED CARDINAL 27

12. BLAZING STAR 29

13. HARDY HIBISCUS 31

14. COMMON YARROW 33

15. SNEEZEWEED 35

16. IMPATIENS 37

17. TIGER LILY 39

18. ASTER 41

19. POINSETTIA 43

20. ORCHID 45

21. TULIP 47

22. FREESIA 49

23. VIOLET 51

24. CROCUS 53

25. BEGONIA 55

26. SNAPDRAGON 57

27. ZINNIA 59

28. DAHLIA 61

29. GARDENIA 63

30. MARIGOLD 65

31. CHRYSANTHEMUM 67

32. ROSE 69

33. LAVENDER 71

34. AZALEA 73

35. CARNATION 75

36. PETUNIA 77

SOLAR SENSATION

Young sunflowers exhibit a phenomenon called "heliotropism," where the flowers follow the direction of the sun throughout the day. Once they reach maturity, sunflowers stop moving and stay facing east until they are harvested.

1. SUNFLOWER

Its name says it all! The sunflower is large, yellow, and brightens the world around us, just like the sun! Native to North America, this flower has been an iconic species for centuries and comes in a variety of colors. The most notable color is yellow, but red, purple, and orange sunflowers are equally stunning. Each flower's head is made up of hundreds to thousands of smaller flowers, each producing a seed. The seeds can be harvested for food and are thought to have been cultivated in America by native peoples even before corn and beans. Today's top-producing sunflower state is North Dakota, while Ukraine and Russia are the top world producers.

CLASSIFICATION

KINGDOM: *Plantae*

CLADE: *Tracheophytes*

CLADE: *Angiosperms*

CLADE: *Eudicots*

CLADE: *Asterids*

ORDER: *Asterales*

FAMILY: *Asteraceae*

GENUS: *Helianthus*

SPECIES: *H. annuus*

BY THE NUMBERS

2,000	*greatest number of seeds a sunflower may contain*
70	*the number of sunflower species*
30	*height in feet of the tallest sunflower*

BETTER BUTTER

As food allergies have become more common, more alternatives to peanut butter are needed. One solution is SunButter! It started in 2002 with cooperation from the U.S. Department of Agriculture to make a peanut butter substitute out of sunflower seeds.

Iris Florentina

DID YOU KNOW?

Are you up for some iris trivia? Tennessee has named the bearded iris its state flower. Meanwhile, the common decorative symbol, the fleur-de-lys, is also an iris. If you ever visit New Orleans, keep an eye out for the fleur-de-lis around the city on flags and buildings, as it is the city's chosen symbol.

2. IRIS

Irises are perennial flowering plants that have been cultivated for thousands of years. Most of the almost 300 iris species originated in the temperate parts of Europe and Asia, but nearly 30 are native to North America. Found in every continental U.S. state and Alaska, most varieties inhabit the Pacific Coast region and the Southeastern United States. You can spot an iris from its three upward-pointing petals and three downward-looking petals, called "sepals." Blooms last about three days, with each stem producing about 10 flowering buds. With incredible diversity in color and striking beauty, it's no wonder that irises are a gardener's delight!

CLASSIFICATION

KINGDOM: *Plantae*

CLADE: *Tracheophytes*

CLADE: *Angiosperms*

CLADE: *Monocots*

ORDER: *Asparagales*

FAMILY: *Iridaceae*

SUBFAMILY: *Iridoideae*

TRIBE: *Irideae*

GENUS: *Iris*

BY THE NUMBERS

3	*number of days the blooms last*
3	*average height of an iris plant in feet*
3	*groups of irises (dwarf, intermediate, and tall)*

Siberian Iris

GREEK MYTHOLOGY

The iris flower is named after the goddess of rainbows, Iris, in Greek mythology. In fact, the word "rainbow" in Greek translates to "iris." Therefore, the flower's name refers to its ability to produce flowers of various colors (similar to a rainbow).

Butterfly
Milkweed

WAR EFFORT

During World War II, the common supply source for life jacket filling was cut off. As a result, milkweed floss was used as a substitute. Children of the day were encouraged to collect milkweed because it was both waterproof and buoyant in life jackets. Two bags of milkweed floss could fill one life jacket.

3. MILKWEED

North America is home to more than 100 species of milkweed, most of which are native to the United States. Its name comes from the milky sap contained in its stems and leaves. While the sap is poisonous and undesirable to herbivores, it is safe for human consumption after being boiled for at least 3 hours. The most well-known trait of the milkweed, besides its lovely perennial bloom clusters, is its benefit to monarch butterflies. Milkweeds are the only plant that monarch caterpillars will eat. In fact, the toxins of the milkweed will remain through the metamorphosis process, providing the newly formed butterfly with protection from predators like birds.

CLASSIFICATION

KINGDOM: *Plantae*

CLADE: *Tracheophytes*

CLADE: *Angiosperms*

CLADE: *Eudicots*

CLADE: *Asterids*

ORDER: *Gentianales*

FAMILY: *Apocynaceae*

SUBFAMILY: *Asclepiadoideae*

TRIBE: *Asclepiadeae*

SUBTRIBE: *Asclepiadinae*

GENUS: *Asclepias*

BY THE NUMBERS

5	height the plant can reach in feet
25	lifespan in years in the wild
11	millions of pounds of milkweed collected for the WWII effort

Showy milkweed

WEIGHTIER MATTERS

While the name milkweed has the word "weed" in it, don't be fooled. It is not a noxious weed but a wildflower with great potential for human benefit. Milkweed floss is being studied as a potential substitution for down feathers in jackets and coats, as it is six times warmer than wool!

SIGNIFICANT SYMBOLISM

Hydrangeas come in a handful of colors, each a symbol of unique expression. Red flowers represent love and gratitude, while pink symbolizes heartfelt emotions like romance. White stands for purity and grace, and blue shows a sense of apology. Lastly, the purple hydrangea displays a deep desire to understand someone.

French
Hydrangea

4. HYDRANGEA

While history shows that hydrangeas were first cultivated in Japan, the flower species is native to both America and Asia. This flowering shrub has flowers that are either pom-pom shaped, known as "mopheads," or flat-headed, known as "lacecaps." Either one, however, will bring a "wow" factor to your garden, even if not all varieties are fragrant. Large, vibrant clusters of these flowers bloom from early spring to late fall. Hydrangeas exhibit an interesting trait—the color of their flowers is largely determined by the pH level of their soil. Sepals turn blue if the pH is less than 5.5, while pink requires a pH level of 7.0.

CLASSIFICATION

KINGDOM: *Plantae*

CLADE: *Tracheophytes*

CLADE: *Angiosperms*

CLADE: *Eudicots*

CLADE: *Asterids*

ORDER: *Cornales*

FAMILY: *Hydrangeaceae*

GENUS: *Hydrangea*

BY THE NUMBERS

5TH	the day in January dedicated to hydrangeas
70+	*species of hydrangea*
4TH	*the marriage anniversary year that is celebrated with hydrangeas*

Panicled Hydrangea

POLLEN PROBLEMS?

If you or someone you know is prone to flower allergies, then hydrangeas are sure to top your favorite flower list! These low-pollen blooms are hypoallergenic and help keep sneezing to a minimum!

13

Great
White
Trillium

SEED SPREADERS

When thinking about pollination, it is common to think of bees and butterflies. Did you know that ants are pollinators too?! Ants enjoy the protein-rich structures, called "elaiosomes," that are attached to the trillium seeds. They will carry them back to their nests, and after taking what they want, the unharmed seeds are discarded to grow a new plant.

5. TRILLIUM

Trillium plants make their home in the deciduous and mixed upland forests of the Eastern United States and Canada. The "tri-" in their name refers to the distinguishing trait of having most of their parts come in sets of three: three broad leaves on a stalk, three petals, and three pollen receptors. Besides being a favorite snack for white-tailed deer, trillium plants are slow-growing perennials. The first brilliant white trillium blooms take 10 years to blossom and only last about three weeks! Similar to sunflowers, trilliums are "phototropic" plants, with blooms that bend toward the sun as it passes across the sky.

CLASSIFICATION

KINGDOM: *Plantae*

CLADE: *Tracheophytes*

CLADE: *Angiosperms*

CLADE: *Monocots*

ORDER: *Liliales*

FAMILY: *Melanthiaceae*

TRIBE: *Parideae*

GENUS: *Trillium*

BY THE NUMBERS

49	*species of trillium in the world (39 in North America)*
25	*years they can survive in the wild*
16	*average number of seeds in each flower*

Toadshade

HANDS OFF!

Early spring is a critical time for trillium plants. They bloom before trees grow leaves in order to capture more sunlight and nutrients to survive the year ahead. If the blooms are picked, the plant may not get all the nutrients it needs and may never fully recover.

TREATMENT FOR TOUGH TIMES

If you have ever wondered what to do for a friend who is having a difficult time, the gift of flowers might be the answer! There is a language to flowers, like roses being a symbol of love. Black-eyed Susans are a symbol of encouragement and justice, inspiring motivation and positive change.

6. BLACK-EYED SUSAN

Black-eyed Susan is an easy-to-spot herbaceous plant that populates open woodlands, fields, and prairies throughout North America. It also makes a lovely addition to gardens with its bright yellow petals surrounding the dark brown, dome-shaped center. Being low-maintenance, fast-growing, and drought-resistant, gardeners are sure to have success cultivating the black-eyed Susan. While they are hardy and bloom profusely in the summer and early fall, black-eyed Susans can spread quickly and are even considered a weed in some places. Excessive spreading can be curtailed by dividing the plant every 3-4 years. Blooms will bring many pollinators to help your garden grow, and the flowers will reseed themselves!

CLASSIFICATION

KINGDOM: *Plantae*

CLADE: *Tracheophytes*

CLADE: *Angiosperms*

CLADE: *Eudicots*

CLADE: *Asterids*

ORDER: *Asterales*

FAMILY: *Asteraceae*

GENUS: *Rudbeckia*

SPECIES: *R. hirta*

BY THE NUMBERS

1918	*the year it become the state flower of Maryland, U.S.*
39	*height the plant can reach in inches*
20	*the greatest number of petals on a flower*

OFFICIAL ORIGIN

While black-eyed Susan flowers originate in North America, their genus name stems from Europe in the 1700s. Carl Linnaeus, a legendary botanist, coined the name after his mentor, Olaf Rudbeck, naming the flower Rudbeckia.

CLOSING TIME

California poppies have their own inner clocks. Their petals close at night and open in the morning. Early Spaniards of California noticed this pattern and gave them the name "dormidera," which means "to fall asleep." Petals will also close in cloudy weather.

7. CALIFORNIA POPPY

The key to a happy California poppy is lots of California sunshine! These vibrant orange beauties are iconic to California but can be found in most of the Western United States. In elevations up to 2,500 meters, they thrive with their petals open to the sun for at least 6 hours a day. With California often lacking excess rainfall, poppies are resilient and drought tolerant, needing only the occasional rainfall. They can also grow in low-quality soil, adding to the beauty of an arid climate in high deserts. Although they are self-seeding, they are visited by many pollinating insects, bringing variety to their surroundings.

CLASSIFICATION

KINGDOM: *Plantae*

CLADE: *Tracheophytes*

CLADE: *Angiosperms*

CLADE: *Eudicots*

ORDER: *Ranunculales*

FAMILY: *Papaveraceae*

GENUS: *Eschscholzia*

SPECIES: *E. californica*

BY THE NUMBERS

1903	*the year it became California's state flower*
1	*number of flowers per stem*
4	*number of petals per flower*

POPULOUS POPPIES

The Antelope Valley California Poppy Reserve is the best place to see the California poppy in full display! Located in the high desert near Lancaster, California, the reserve boasts 1,700 acres of poppy fields with other wildflowers as well! This protected land is left completely to nature, devoid of any man-made water or stimulating sources for the flowers.

PERSONAL SPACE

Gardeners who plant woodland phlox understand the plant's need for growing room. Individual plants need to be spaced about 15 inches apart, as they will grow into the space, emerging larger each year.

8. WOODLAND PHLOX

If "woodland phlox" sounds unfamiliar, this semi-green perennial also goes by the names "wild blue phlox" or "wild sweet William." Home to the eastern half of North America and parts of Canada, this flower boasts a striking blue or violet color with white shading near its stamen. Its natural habitat, as its name implies, is the low woodlands, where sunlight streams through the large trees around it. Such partial shade is necessary for the flowers to thrive as they spread across the woodland floor, creating large drifts of flowers. Look for the beautiful blooms to last for a month in early spring!

CLASSIFICATION

KINGDOM: *Plantae*

CLADE: *Tracheophytes*

CLADE: *Angiosperms*

CLADE: *Eudicots*

CLADE: *Asterids*

ORDER: *Ericales*

FAMILY: *Polemoniaceae*

GENUS: *Phlox*

SPECIES: *P. divaricata*

BY THE NUMBERS

65	the number of phlox species
5	number of petals per flower
12	inches in height of a mature phlox plant

BUTTERFLIES WANTED!

Phlox plants require cross-pollination to produce seeds, and butterflies make the best pollinators! Unlike some insects, butterflies have a long proboscis to reach the flower's nectar. As they sip nectar, their anthers pick up pollen that will transfer to the stigma of the next flower, aiding in pollination.

Indian Blanketflower

ANCIENT FOLKLORE

Legend has it that the origin of the blanket flower dates back to the native Aztecs. The original yellow flower changed after the Spanish conquered Mexico, bringing death and ruin—the new red around the base of the petals symbolized the blood of the fallen Aztec people.

9. BLANKET FLOWER

Gaillardias (or "blanket flowers") were named after the French magistrate Gaillard de Charentonneau, who was a botany enthusiast. Its common name, however, comes from the flowers' similarities to the brightly patterned blankets made by Native Americans. This drought-tolerant perennial is native to both North and South America and is a member of the sunflower family. Blanket flowers are easy to spot with their showy colors of red, yellow, and orange, along with their 3-lobed petals, which differ from those of a typical sunflower. Due to their vibrant appearance, blanket flowers are widely dried and preserved for potpourri and flower arrangements.

GO BOBCATS!

Texas State University has a direct connection with the blanket flower. The school colors of maroon and gold were inspired by the Gaillardia, or blanket flower, which grows wild across the plains of Texas.

CLASSIFICATION

KINGDOM: *Plantae*

CLADE: *Tracheophytes*

CLADE: *Angiosperms*

CLADE: *Eudicots*

CLADE: *Asterids*

ORDER: *Asterales*

FAMILY: *Asteraceae*

SUBFAMILY: *Asteroideae*

TRIBE: *Helenieae*

SUBTRIBE: *Gaillardiinae*

GENUS: *Gaillardia*

BY THE NUMBERS

1788	*the year the species was discovered*
3	*inches the flowers can reach in diameter*
1986	*the year the blanket flower became the official wildflower for the state of Oklahoma*

Purple
Coneflower

TIED TO THE OCEAN

The Latin name for the coneflower genus is Echinacea. The Latin "echinos" means "sea urchin," which refers to the spiky texture of the coneflower's cone. An alternate meaning is "hedgehog," which also aptly describes the prickly cone.

10. CONEFLOWER

As members of the daisy family, it's no wonder coneflowers resemble daisies with their slender petals and long stems. The main difference in appearance is that coneflowers have a large, dome-shaped center called a "cone," which is made up of hundreds of small florets. The petals themselves seem to droop beneath the cone, setting it apart from the perky daisy. These native wildflowers flourish in the prairies and grasslands of the eastern and central parts of North America, where they are initially odorless. As they age, coneflowers release a honey-like scent that draws plenty of pollinators. After pollination, the coneflowers emit a sweet, vanilla-like aroma.

BY THE NUMBERS

4	*height in feet its hairy stem can grow*
9	*the number of coneflower species*
5	*lifespan in years in the wild*

Cutleaf Coneflower

HEALTH BENEFITS

Echinacea, as it is referred to in the health and medical fields, is another word for coneflowers. The leaves, roots, and flowering tops of three of the nine species are commonly used in herbal medicine. Echinacea is used to strengthen the body's immune system and help fight illness.

LOVE CHARM

The Pawnee is a Native American tribe that inhabits the Central Plains of the United States. They believed that the red cardinal flower held special powers as a love charm. Possession of the plant was thought to make you irresistible to the one you loved.

11. RED CARDINAL

Though they bloom in late summer, red cardinals are worth the wait! These flowers are deep-red, short-lived perennials that add a burst of color to gardens and low woodlands alike. The species is found as far north as Canada and as far south as parts of Northern Columbia. As self-seeding flowers, red cardinals grow quickly and depend on moist soil to survive. These tubular flowers can appear in clusters on the main stem and provide needed habitat for butterflies and moths. Such pollinators lay their eggs on the cardinal flowers, and when they hatch, the caterpillars and moths will stay on the cardinal leaves.

CLASSIFICATION

KINGDOM: *Plantae*

CLADE: *Tracheophytes*

CLADE: *Angiosperms*

CLADE: *Eudicots*

CLADE: *Rosids*

ORDER: *Fabales*

FAMILY: *Fabaceae*

SUBFAMILY: *Faboideae*

GENUS: *Erythrina*

SPECIES: *E. herbacea*

BY THE NUMBERS

5	total petals per flower (2 upper and 3 lower)
4	height the plant can reach in feet
3	lifespan in years in the wild

HUMMINGBIRD HELP

If the red cardinal flower gave an MVP award for pollination, the hummingbird would be the recipient! With long flowers, the hummingbird is the primary pollinator of the red cardinal, using its long, thin beak to reach the nectar.

Prairie Blazing Star

UNUSUAL GROWTH

Unlike many flowers, blazing stars bloom from the top down as opposed to the bottom up. As a result, blazing stars make a great cut flower! When blooms look tired, they can be cut off, and the stalk will still continue to produce new blooms further down the stem.

12. BLAZING STAR

Liatris is the scientific name for "blazing stars," a true prairie flower native to North America. As prairie flowers, they can grow in poor soil conditions while sailing through summers of heat and drought. Their normal appearance is unassuming, with tall green stalks and almost grass-like leaves. The real show takes place from July to October, when the wildflowers are born! Showy spikes of pink, purple, or white flowers bloom in clumps on the long stalks. The feathery texture of the blooms gives them the nickname "gayfeather." A beautiful contrast to any garden, the blazing star provides a prevalent resting spot or pollination stop for songbirds, butterflies, and honeybees.

CLASSIFICATION

KINGDOM: *Plantae*

CLADE: *Tracheophytes*

CLADE: *Angiosperms*

CLADE: *Eudicots*

CLADE: *Asterids*

ORDER: *Asterales*

FAMILY: *Asteraceae*

SUBFAMILY: *Asteroideae*

TRIBE: *Eupatorieae*

GENUS: *Liatris*

BY THE NUMBERS

18	*distance in inches plants should be placed apart*
3	*height in feet at maturity*
40+	*number of blazing star species*

Dense Blazing Star

WATER WISE

While all plants depend on water, too much is detrimental to blazing stars. Moist and well-drained soil are needed to prevent rot in the "corms" (the modified storage root resembling a bulb). Poor soil is not a problem for blazing stars—just soggy soil!

PATIENCE NEEDED

Careful planning and research are important for the successful cultivation of the hardy hibiscus. Poor soil will need compost added, and full sun is needed for maximum bloom (but only up to 6 hours of exposure). Roots need to stay moist, and adding mulch is helpful. Hardy hibiscus also benefits from fertilizing. However, too much can lead to toxicity.

13. HARDY HIBISCUS

Need a splash of color or some tropical flair to add to your perennial garden? If so, hardy hibiscus might just be the solution. While they can be confused with their tropical cousins, hardy hibiscus is a North American native that resembles Hawaii's state flower. Both varieties show a prominent staminal column, giving them extra dimension. The hardy hibiscus boasts five-petaled flowers that are the largest perennial flowers in North America. Their love of moist, rich soil is shown in their natural habitat near rivers and wetlands in the Eastern United States. These eye-popping flowers come in white, red, pink, and blue!

BY THE NUMBERS

8	height the plant can grow in feet
12	diameter in inches a flower can grow
-30	temperature in Fahrenheit the plant can survive

LATE BLOOMER

As spring approaches, you might be concerned about your hardy hibiscus plant. Don't worry, it's not dead! It is characteristic of the genus to come out of dormancy late in the season. Once they awake, they can grow more than an inch a day!

MEDICINAL REMEDIES

People of the Cherokee tribe took advantage of the healing properties of the yarrow plant. Natives concocted a yarrow tea steep that worked as a sleep aid and fever reducer. One cup of hot water was combined with 1-2 teaspoons of the dried herb. After straining and cooling, the tea was to be consumed three times a day.

14. COMMON YARROW

The common yarrow is a familiar species to both gardeners and outdoor enthusiasts like hikers. With widespread distribution throughout North America and Asia, the yarrow is known as an attractive perennial with dome-shaped clusters of white, pink, or red flowers. Their home is found in almost all climates, from coastal regions and mountains to the driest deserts. Yarrow reproduces quickly and can easily spread through its self-sowing and underground stems, sometimes acting as an invasive flowering plant. The yarrow is a spring bloomer that attracts various pollinators and has an aromatic scent similar to the chrysanthemum. In addition to providing many health benefits, common yarrow also helps to improve soil conditions and lower the risk of erosion.

CLASSIFICATION

KINGDOM: *Plantae*

CLADE: *Tracheophytes*

CLADE: *Angiosperms*

CLADE: *Eudicots*

CLADE: *Asterids*

ORDER: *Asterales*

FAMILY: *Asteraceae*

GENUS: *Achillea*

SPECIES: *A. millefolium*

BY THE NUMBERS

3	*height the plant can reach in feet*
4	*width of flower clusters in inches*
2+	*years the yarrow can survive in the wild*

LEGENDARY NAME

The scientific name for yarrow is Achillea millefolium, which is named after Achilles, the Greek war hero. According to folklore, Achilles used the yarrow plant to treat the wounds of his soldiers during the Trojan War.

Basin Sneezeweed

A RARE BEAUTY

*Virginia sneezeweed (Helenium
virginicum) is one of 40 sneezeweed
species and the only one endemic to
Virginia in the United States. It is
considered a rare perennial wildflower
that was first discovered in 1936. It is
federally protected as it is currently
threatened as an endangered species.*

15. SNEEZEWEED

Despite what its curious name suggests, the perennial sneezeweed produces both lovely and charming flowers that come in shades of red, yellow, orange, and brown. Another common name for sneezeweed is Helenium, originating from Greek mythology. Legend has it that sneezeweed grew out of the ground after being soaked in the tears of Helen of Troy. These daisy-like flowers are made up of long, three-lobed petals surrounding the base of a central dome. "Florets," or smaller disk flowers, are what make up the center. Sneezeweed can be found all over North America (minus parts of the tundra) in areas of moist soil and full sun exposure. Due to their (almost) 5-foot height, the plant may need staking for support.

CLASSIFICATION

KINGDOM: *Plantae*

CLADE: *Tracheophytes*

CLADE: *Angiosperms*

CLADE: *Eudicots*

CLADE: *Asterids*

ORDER: *Asterales*

FAMILY: *Asteraceae*

SUBFAMILY: *Asteroideae*

TRIBE: *Helenieae*

SUBTRIBE: *Gaillardiinae*

GENUS: *Helenium*

BY THE NUMBERS

2	*lifespan in weeks of cut flowers*
3	*width of the plant in feet*
5	*normal lifespan in years in the wild*

Orange Sneezeweed

BLESS YOU!

Despite its name, sneezeweed flower pollen does not induce sneezing! The name was given due to the ancient use of the dried leaves to make snuff (smokeless tobacco), which made you sneeze with inhalation. Its purpose was to rid the body of evil spirits.

FOR REAL?

Nature can surely keep us on our toes with so many interesting plant characteristics! Over the course of their lives, some impatiens change their sex. The flower is male when it first blooms. Once the pollen cap disappears a few days later, the female organs appear!

16. IMPATIENS

Questions arise when you stop to think about how impatiens got their name. Also known as "touch-me-nots," impatiens are aptly named for the super-sensitive, mature seed capsules that will burst when lightly touched. This "explosion" sends seeds flying through the air and is quite a sight to behold! Impatiens is a huge genus with over 1,000 species, most of which are annual plants outside the tropics. They are widely found throughout Asia, Africa, and North America as one of the most popular annual garden bed plants. As a shade-loving ground cover, impatiens come in blue, orange, pink, purple, red, white, and bicolor varieties.

BY THE NUMBERS

1	*days the flower will last*
8	*garden spacing in inches*
5	*number of petals per flower*

BUSY LIZZY

"Busy Lizzy" is another name used for impatiens to describe their prolific blooming! They can have single, semi-double, and double blooms from early summer to fall. All is well until the first frost, when the plant will turn to mush.

WILD AND HAPPY

Tiger lilies are easy-to-grow perennial flowers that are hardy and heat-tolerant. They are sometimes referred to as "trench lilies," as they can be seen growing wild in ditches. Moist soils are where they are most happy, without the need for special care.

17. TIGER LILY

W hile they don't have sharp teeth or purr, tiger lily flowers do have some similarities to the animal that inspired their name. Tiger lilies have unique and bold orange flowers with black spots, similar to the fiery tiger. Naturalized in eastern parts of North America, the tiger lily is native to parts of Asia and the Russian Far East. Part of the dramatic appearance of the tiger lily sets it apart from other flowers. Its six curled petals and six tall stamens provide a uniquely dainty look, and they grow taller and larger each year!

FLOWERS AND FONDANT

Everyone appreciates a gorgeous wedding cake decorated with flowers to add beauty to the occasion. Did you know that you can enjoy your fondant with flowers and eat them too?! Tiger lilies are edible and, therefore, a great choice for cake decorations!

New England
Aster

UNSOLVED MYSTERY

Why is it that asters close their flowers at night and on cold and rainy days yet open again in the morning? Though it has not been scientifically proven, the prevailing thought is that the aster is trying to protect its pollen from moisture in order to maintain viability.

18. ASTER

As one of the fall's last blooming flowers, the aster is a terrific addition to any garden. Also known as "keystone plants," asters bring a multitude of pollinators! To 112 species of moths and butterflies, they are known as host plants and provide much-needed nutrients for caterpillars. They can be found growing wildly in dense clumps in meadows, fens, prairies, and forest edges. While the plant can have a scraggly appearance, the charming flowers make up the difference. Many thin petals around the central dome of "florets" (smaller flowers) give them the name "ray flowers." Purple is the predominant petal color of the species.

CLASSIFICATION

KINGDOM: *Plantae*

CLADE: *Tracheophytes*

CLADE: *Angiosperms*

CLADE: *Eudicots*

CLADE: *Asterids*

ORDER: *Asterales*

FAMILY: *Asteraceae*

SUBFAMILY: *Asteroideae*

TRIBE: *Astereae*

SUBTRIBE: *Asterinae*

GENUS: *Aster*

BY THE NUMBERS

100+	*number of small florets in each flower*
3	*months of bloom*
4	*common plant height in feet in the wild*

Tatarian Aster

RESOURCEFUL REMEDIES

Native Americans had countless uses for the aster plant. The Chippewa attracted wild game by smoking the roots in pipes, while the Meskwaki used their heavy smell to revive unconscious people. In addition, the Cherokee people used the aster plant to help reduce fevers.

MYTH BUSTER

The common belief that poinsettias are poisonous is incorrect. While its milky white sap can cause skin irritations in humans and pets, it is not toxic. While consuming a poinsettia won't kill you, your tastebuds will surely be angry at the awful taste!

19. POINSETTIA

It might be mind-blowing, but not all poinsettias are red! Native to Mexico and Central America, poinsettias are perennial plants that come in over 100 varieties, including colors of red, pink, white, and burgundy; they can even be marbled and speckled. It might also be mind-blowing that the lovely "petals" are not flowers but leaves! The real flowers are the tiny yellow buds in the center of each "bract" (or group of leaves). Associated with the Christmas season, the poinsettia market only lasts about 6 weeks yet yields an impressive economic impact. The season brings in about $1 billion in annual sales worldwide.

CLASSIFICATION

KINGDOM: *Plantae*

CLADE: *Tracheophytes*

CLADE: *Angiosperms*

CLADE: *Eudicots*

CLADE: *Rosids*

ORDER: *Malpighiales*

FAMILY: *Euphorbiaceae*

GENUS: *Euphorbia*

SPECIES: *E. pulcherrima*

BY THE NUMBERS

1825	the year the flower was named after Joel Poinsett, who introduced the flower to the U.S.
15	height in feet they can reach in the wild as a woody shrub
12	the day in December known as National Poinsettia Day

TRADITIONAL TALE

Christmas poinsettias come from a Mexican tale of a poor child who gathered weeds from the roadside as his humble gift to place on the altar of the church on Christmas Eve. As members of the congregation watched, the weeds transformed into brilliant red and green flowers.

Dancing-Lady
Orchid

UP FOR A CHALLENGE?

*Orchids can be prolific bloomers
once they are mature. However,
patience is required to be
a successful cultivator. The
first flowers won't appear
for about 5-7 years. To put it
in perspective, store-bought
orchids are almost a decade old!*

20. ORCHID

As the largest family of flowering plants, orchids have immense diversity among their species. They are believed to be the oldest flowering plant on Earth and can be found worldwide. As a result, the orchid has various meanings and cultural significance depending on where it is located on the globe. For instance, in Chinese tradition, orchids represent good taste, beauty, and refinement. A sure way to identify an orchid is to notice its symmetry. Each flower can be divided perfectly in half, like looking at a mirror image. It can be compared to the symmetry of the human face.

CLASSIFICATION

KINGDOM: *Plantae*

CLADE: *Tracheophytes*

CLADE: *Angiosperms*

CLADE: *Monocots*

ORDER: *Asparagales*

FAMILY: *Orchidaceae*

BY THE NUMBERS

100	*greatest age it can reach in years*
25,000+	*species of orchid in the world*
3	*millions of seeds in one orchid seed pod*

Egg-in-a-Nest Orchid

BAKING NECESSITY

When it comes to baking necessities, vanilla extract is a must! The dark brown, long, and thin bean pod is actually the fruit of an orchid plant! Vanilla planifolia is the orchid species that produces 99% of commercial vanilla.

TULIP MANIA

"Tulip mania" was a real term in Holland during the mid-1600s. Speculation had driven the price of bulbs to the extreme, with the rarest tulip bulb trading as high as six times the average person's annual salary. This famous market bubble did crash, but it served as one of the most infamous asset bubbles/crashes of all time.

21. TULIP

With a uniquely symmetrical shape and blooms that come in almost any color, tulips are a garden standout! Loved by flower enthusiasts everywhere, tulips are a sign of spring's arrival and rebirth. They are cultivated worldwide with more than 3,000 varieties, including the "Queen of the Night" tulip, which boasts dark purple petals that look almost black. Festivals are held all over the United States to celebrate tulips, despite the fact that the blooms only last around a week. Besides their beauty, tulips are a resourceful flowering plant to have on hand. The petals are a lovely addition to a spring salad, while the tulip bulb can serve as a substitute for an onion.

CLASSIFICATION

KINGDOM: *Plantae*

CLADE: *Tracheophytes*

CLADE: *Angiosperms*

CLADE: *Monocots*

ORDER: *Liliales*

FAMILY: *Liliaceae*

SUBFAMILY: *Lilioideae*

TRIBE: *Lilieae*

GENUS: *Tulipa*

BY THE NUMBERS

3	*billions of tulip bulbs exported annually from the Netherlands*
2	*the second most popular flower on Valentine's Day*
150	*the number of tulip species*

UNLIKELY ORIGIN

For many, the word "tulip" is synonymous with Holland, as the Netherlands is the tulip capital of the world. Surprisingly, tulips were not introduced in Holland until the 1560s. They originated in central Asia and were first sent to Turkey; from there, they were sent to Holland.

FOREVER FRIENDS

The freesia got its name from German botanist Christian P. Ecklon, who named the bloom after his close friend and fellow botanist, Dr. Friedrich Freese. As a result, the freesia came to symbolize lasting friendships.

22. FREESIA

Weddings are a common place to see cut freesias! Their delicate appearance of tiny blooms on a slender stalk is a subtle complement to more showy flowers like roses and peonies. Offering plenty of variation, freesia can be white, pink, red, or yellow (the most aromatic being the red and pink flowers). Due to their fragrant aroma, freesias are commonly used in lotions, perfumes, soaps, and other cosmetic products. Though highly desirable, freesias can be temperamental. They are native to tropical areas of South Africa and thrive in mild winters, but they go dormant in summers. Temperatures have to be lower than 70 degrees Fahrenheit for flowers to bloom.

BY THE NUMBERS

7	the wedding anniversary year the flower represents
16+	species of freesia (though 300+ hybrids exist)
8	common number of blooms per stalk

NEW VOCABULARY

Freesias are "zygomorphic." What is the meaning of such a fancy world? Simply put, it means that the blooms of the freesia plant only grow on one side of the stalk.

Bird's Foot Violet

FLOWER FANATIC

The French military commander and politician, Napoleon Bonaparte, was a violet devotee. To his soldiers, he was nicknamed "Corporal Violet," and he even used his signature flowers to cover the grave of his wife, Josephine, in 1814.

23. VIOLET

Being the state flower of Wisconsin, New Jersey, Illinois, and Rhode Island, it may not come as a surprise that violets thrive in shady, cool climates (not to be confused with African violets, which require warmer weather). Moist soil is a must. Their most dominant colors are blue and purple, though they can also exhibit white and multicolored flowers. Also known as "viola" in Latin, violets are one of the most popular flowers for perfumery worldwide. Though violets may resemble pansy flowers, take a close look at their leaves. Violet leaves are usually heart-shaped and are either smooth or covered in fine hairs.

CLASSIFICATION

KINGDOM: *Plantae*

CLADE: *Tracheophytes*

CLADE: *Angiosperms*

CLADE: *Eudicots*

CLADE: *Rosids*

ORDER: *Malpighiales*

FAMILY: *Violaceae*

SUBFAMILY: *Violoideae*

TRIBE: *Violeae*

GENUS: *Viola*

BY THE NUMBERS

5	*number of petals and sepals per flower*
1907	*the year school children in Illinois voted to make the violet the state flower*
500	*the year BC that the flowers date back to in Greece*

Sweet Violet

ELEGANT AND ELUSIVE

Besides being known for their beauty, violets are known for their lovely scent. The only problem is that the aroma seems to disappear readily after sniffing. This is caused by the chemical ionone, which temporarily desensitizes the nose and sense of smell.

SCATTERING SUNSHINE

For many, the crocus flower has long symbolized cheerfulness and youthfulness. However, it is also referred to as the "light bulb flower." Until the petals unfurl into the familiar cup-shaped flower, the crocus bulb resembles the well-known shape of the light bulb.

24. CROCUS

Crocuses are perennial plants that belong to the Iris family. They grow from bulbs and were originally found in southern Europe, Asia, Africa, and the Middle East. Today, crocuses can be found worldwide on rocky mountainsides, woodlands, and scrublands, where they can tolerate cold climates. In areas of high altitude, the bright flowers of the crocus can poke out of the snow, signifying that winter is coming to an end. These cup-shaped flowers bloom in white, lilac, lavender, yellow, and mauve; they can also be striped. Crocus flowers are characterized by their six petals, but the central white stripes on the leaves of the plant are sure to give away their identity!

CLASSIFICATION

KINGDOM: *Plantae*

CLADE: *Tracheophytes*

CLADE: *Angiosperms*

CLADE: *Monocots*

ORDER: *Asparagales*

FAMILY: *Iridaceae*

SUBFAMILY: *Crocoideae*

TRIBE: *Ixieae*

GENUS: *Crocus*

BY THE NUMBERS

12	*height of the plant in inches*
80+	*the number of crocus species*
3	*number of stigmas per flower*

EXPENSIVE TASTE

The world's most expensive spice by weight is saffron. It is harvested by hand from the red stigmas of Crocus sativus flowers and is popular in many Mediterranean, Indian, and Middle Eastern dishes. Producing an ounce of saffron requires about 1,000 flowers.

BRING ON THE HEAT

While begonias cannot tolerate freezing temperatures, they are not afraid of the heat! Thanks to their succulent-like stems, begonias can store water, making them drought-tolerant.

25. BEGONIA

Begonias are a perennial garden favorite because of their reputation for being low-maintenance. Growing naturally in tropical and subtropical environments, begonias thrive in warm climates with partial shade. If these needs are met, begonias won't need a lot of attention. Whether indoors or outdoors, begonias can display single or double blooms of red, pink, white, and yellow. Usually compact in size, begonia plants have dense foliage and can grow well in containers and in masses in flower beds. In the floral dictionary, "begonia" means "be cautious," and in ancient times, the plant was used to polish sword blades.

KINGDOM: *Plantae*

CLADE: *Tracheophytes*

CLADE: *Angiosperms*

CLADE: *Eudicots*

CLADE: *Rosids*

ORDER: *Cucurbitales*

FAMILY: *Begoniaceae*

GENUS: *Begonia*

BY THE NUMBERS

40	*highest percentage of humidity required by begonias*
1,500+	*the number of begonia species*
1	*average height of the plant in feet*

SMALL BUT MIGHTY

Begonias are proof that power can come in small packages. Though they produce the smallest seeds in the world of flowers, a tiny amount can go a long way. As many as 3 million seedlings can grow from a single ounce of begonia seeds.

Snapdragons are a flower species susceptible to ethylene gas. Such gases come from external sources like ripening fruit and excess heat. The result can lead to the wilting and early death of snapdragons. Next time you're tempted to put your lovely vase of flowers beside your kitchen fruit basket, think again!

26. SNAPDRAGON

Snapdragons have been cultivated since the 1700s and are native to North Africa, the United States, and rocky areas of Europe. It wasn't until the 1950s that the flowers were hybridized. Today, around 40 species of snapdragons exist. Blooms can be green, red, yellow, pink, or white as they grow along the soft green stalks, producing best in the cooler temperatures of spring and fall. Similar to other flower species, snapdragons are edible and make an attractive garnish. Their curious name comes from the way the flower opens like a dragon's mouth when you pinch the base of the flower. Give it a try!

BY THE NUMBERS

10	*the average number of days the flowers will last before wilting*
6	*height in inches of the smallest snapdragon variety*
15	*the greatest number of blooms per stalk*

HANDFUL OF CHOICES

Snapdragons come in five size varieties to meet the needs of your garden. Your options are tall, intermediate, short, dwarf, and trailing. For garden borders and cutting gardens, the tall snapdragon is recommended. Shorter varieties best suit containers and window boxes.

PERFECT FOR BEGINNERS!

For those just starting to garden, zinnias are a perfect starting point. In fact, upon introduction, Europeans called the zinnia "everybody's flower" and "poorhouse flower" because they were common and easy to grow.

27. ZINNIA

If you are looking for a low-maintenance flowering plant with a wide range of color options, then look no further! Zinnias offer both traits along with a tolerance for the hot climates of their native South America and the Southwestern United States. Though they appear similar in form to daisies, zinnias can exhibit single, semi-double, or double layers of petals. Bright colors like yellow, orange, purple, red, and lilac will attract hummingbirds and butterflies to pollinate your garden. Ironically, these well-known and loved beauties were once seen as repulsive by Spanish explorers, who gave zinnias the name "mal de osos," meaning "sickness of the eye!"

BY THE NUMBERS

2016	*the year the zinnia became the first flower to grow in space*
7	*height in inches of the dwarf zinnia species*
7	*bloom life in days before the cut flowers begin to wilt*

DECISIONS, DECISIONS

When it comes to thinking about next year's garden, you might have a tough choice to make. Zinnias will reseed themselves if the dead flowers are not removed. But pulling off the dead blooms (called deadheading) will increase the number of blooms you get that season. What would you do?

FASCINATING FACTS

There are so many fascinating things to learn about dahlia flowers. From being the favorite flower of Queen Victoria and Marie Antoinette to the official flowers of Seattle and San Francisco, dahlias make their mark around the world! They were even named after the Swedish botanist, Anders Dahl.

28. DAHLIA

Dahlias are part of the Asteraceae family with other flower standouts like asters, sunflowers, daisies, and chrysanthemums. This classification is, in part, due to the appearance of dahlia blooms, which resemble a star surrounded by rays ("Asteraceae" comes from the Greek word for star). Besides coming in almost every color besides blue, dahlias are a fan favorite because their bloom production peaks in mid-summer when other flower species are on their way out. Mountain regions of Guatemala and Mexico are considered the starting place for dahlia flower ancestors; it makes sense that dahlias were named Mexico's national flower in 1963.

CLASSIFICATION

KINGDOM: *Plantae*

CLADE: *Tracheophytes*

CLADE: *Angiosperms*

CLADE: *Eudicots*

CLADE: *Asterids*

ORDER: *Asterales*

FAMILY: *Asteraceae*

SUBFAMILY: *Asteroideae*

TRIBE: *Coreopsideae*

GENUS: *Dahlia*

BY THE NUMBERS

1	*diameter in feet of the largest dahlia flower heads*
42+	*recognized dahlia species*
1615	*the year the dahlia flower was first recorded by Westerners*

EAT YOUR VEGETABLES

It might be interesting to learn that the dahlia plant was originally considered a vegetable in the 18th century because of its edible tubers, or tubular root system. These edible tubers are said to taste like a combination of radishes and potatoes.

FRUIT FACTS

Like all flowering plants, gardenias produce fruit. The fruit of the gardenia flower contains a carotenoid compound called "crocin," which produces a yellow color. It has been used as a yellow dye in paper, leather, foods, cosmetics, and textiles.

29. GARDENIA

Milky white petals with a soft, waxy texture and a sweetly pleasant smell give away the identity of gardenias. Tropical by nature, gardenias are native to certain parts of Hawaii, Africa, and Asia. Full sunlight, acidic soil, and a warm environment allow them to thrive. Surprisingly, not all gardenias are white. One variety, the golden gardenia, produces attractive, flat, yellow blooms. Despite their hard appearance, gardenias are actually quite delicate. Once the flower is cut, the blooms have a short life, especially if touched. Bruising is common on the petals when touched, causing the blooms to turn off-white and darken until they die.

BY THE NUMBERS

5	*maximum diameter of a flower in inches*
3	*the minimum spacing in feet needed when planting gardenias*
250	*the approximate number of gardenia species*

THINGS IN COMMON

Gardenias have something in common with black-eyed Susan flowers. Both were given their genus names by the Scottish botanist, Carl Linnaeus. Alexander Garden, after whom the flower was named, was a Scottish naturalist and physician, as well as a friend of Linnaeus.

MARIGOLDS IN MEXICO

Mexico's Dia de los Muertos, or Day of the Dead, is celebrated on the first two days of November in honor of loved ones who have passed away. Decorations for the celebration usually include fresh or paper-cut marigolds. It is believed that the marigold's strong scent guides the spirits to visit the altars set up on their behalf.

30. MARIGOLD

Marigolds are annual or perennial flowering plants that have a long history of cultivation. Though native to North and South America, marigolds have now naturalized around the globe. Their brilliant hues of deep orange and yellow with occasional maroon highlights are sure to brighten up any garden or mood. Marigold plants can vary in size from under 1 foot tall to over 7 feet, with blooms that can grow singly on a stem or in clusters. The common appearance of marigold plants consists of feather-like leaves and globe-shaped flowers. Look for them in their natural habitat near ponds, streams, and wet meadows.

BY THE NUMBERS

1	lifespan of annual marigold plants in years
36	width the plant can reach in inches
56	the number of marigold species

EXTRACTS FOR EYESIGHT

Lutein is an organic pigment known as a "carotenoid" that is found in the petals of marigolds and is related to beta-carotene and vitamin A. The use of marigold extract, which contains lutein, provides numerous health benefits. Known as "the eye vitamin," lutein can help treat age-related macular degeneration of the eyes.

FESTIVALS AND CELEBRATIONS

Japan is not shy about its love for chrysanthemums. Each year, the flower is celebrated on September 9th for National Chrysanthemum Day, also known as the "Festival of Happiness." The flower has also been used for over 1,200 years as the crest of the emperor.

31.
CHRYSANTHEMUM

Native to Northeastern Europe and Asia, chrysanthemums are ancient tropical flowers that are now cultivated worldwide. Sunny areas with well-drained and fertile soil (whether indoor or outdoor) make growing chrysanthemums a piece of cake. So popular are they that "mums" are one of the most widely sold plants in garden centers between August and November. With thousands of varieties due to selective breeding, chrysanthemums can exhibit great diversity among the species. The most common flower form is the tidy button mum, with tightly packed petals that resemble a pom-pom. Other flower forms include the daisy, spider, fuji, suction, and disbud varieties.

BY THE NUMBERS

.4	*diameter of the smallest variety in inches*
1798	*the year chrysanthemums were imported to the U.S.*
10	*diameter of the largest variety in inches*

TRADITIONAL HUE

Greek history played a part in naming the chrysanthemum flower. The Greek word "chrysos" means "gold," and "anthemon" means "flower." When the two Greek words come together, it sounds a lot like chrysanthemum. The traditional color is yellow or gold, but mums also come in purples, pinks, bronze, white, and red.

WALL OF ROSES

The typical lifespan of a rose plant is around 10 years. However, with the right care, they can last well beyond their life expectancy. The oldest living rose plant is believed to be around 1,000 years old and still grows on the wall of Germany's Hildesheim Cathedral.

32. ROSE

Unequivocally, the rose is the world's most popular flower, and there is way more to them than just being a Valentine's Day staple. With so much diversity among the 300+ species, you are sure to find a variety to please your taste. Roses can grow as shrubs, wall climbers, or groundcovers in six main colors: white, red, orange, pink, yellow, and purple. Cultivated worldwide, the rose has found a sweet spot in the United States. In 1986, the rose was declared the national flower by President Ronald Reagan. In addition, the town of Pasadena, California, holds the iconic Rose Parade every New Year's Day.

CLASSIFICATION

KINGDOM: *Plantae*

CLADE: *Tracheophytes*

CLADE: *Angiosperms*

CLADE: *Eudicots*

CLADE: *Rosids*

ORDER: *Rosales*

FAMILY: *Rosaceae*

SUBFAMILY: *Rosoideae*

TRIBE: *Roseae*

GENUS: *Rosa*

BY THE NUMBERS

4,000+	*number of songs dedicated to roses*
1998	*the year a rose went into space for the first time*
7	*lifespan in days of a cut rose*

TEDIOUS TREASURE

Extracting the essential oils from the flowerheads of roses leads to the creation of lovely and highly sought-after perfumes. Unfortunately, the process is not as pleasant as the scent. Producing one gram of rose oil requires about 2,000 roses.

English Lavender

QUESTIONING COLORS

With the same name as its color, it would be easy to assume that the lavender flower only comes in shades of purple. Remarkably, however, lavender varieties can also come in white, yellow, and pink. Thankfully, the color of the flowers does not affect their scent.

33. LAVENDER

Lavender has ancient roots with centuries of symbolism and uses that make it a well-known flowering plant. Lavender originates from the Mediterranean regions, along with areas of Africa and Asia. Its name comes from the Latin word "lavare," which means "to wash," as it was used in ancient Rome for bathing rituals. In fact, just the thought of lavender might make you take a deep breath and relax. The essential oils of lavender are popular in perfumes and aromatherapy as their scent has a calming effect on most people. The small flowers at the end of long stalks give off a scent that combines the likes of honey, thyme, and balsam fir.

BY THE NUMBERS

450+	*the number of lavender varieties*
2	*second most popular herb worldwide (behind basil)*
45	*the approximate number of lavender species*

English Lavender

FAMOUSLY FAMILIAR

Lavender is everywhere—in shampoos, desserts, perfumes, teas, and scented candles! Evidence of its beneficial uses is far and wide! Unlike the human race, pests such as flies, mosquitoes, and mice hate the smell of lavender. Such repulsiveness is another reason to keep lavender around the house!

WARTIME HOPE

Legend has it that after English travelers brought azaleas to America, they became a symbol of love and hope for wartime families. Wives of traveling soldiers planted yellow azaleas to convey their love for their families and to help cope with the heartache caused by war.

34. AZALEA

Azaleas are flowering shrubs native to Europe, Asia, and America that can be either evergreen or deciduous. Flowers are typically pink, white, or orange, with blooms appearing around May and June. Life in the shade or partial sun is where azaleas thrive. Shallow roots make it necessary to keep the soil moist. Additionally, planting azaleas near conifer trees can be helpful, as the needles and bark act as mulch. Despite their beauty, all parts of the azalea plant are poisonous. Toxins called "grayanotoxins" can disrupt the digestive system and affect heart rate and blood pressure.

BY THE NUMBERS

1	*number of flowers per stem*
1,000+	*number of azalea varieties*
10	*height the shrub can reach in feet*

PETAL POWER

Azalea blooms can vary in size and shape depending on their variety. "Single" flowers have five petals each, while "hose-in-hose" flowers can possess 12. The "double hose-in-hose" flowers can produce over 30 petals. In addition, the petals can be ruffled, flat, or recurved.

RICH HISTORY

Cultivation of the carnation began over 2,000 years ago in the ancient cultures of Greece and Rome. In fact, the Greek translation of its scientific name, dianthus, means "flower of the gods." They were a popular decorative choice in many ceremonial coronations, which is where the name "carnation" was born.

35. CARNATION

Popular is an understatement when it comes to describing carnations. Having been around for centuries, carnations have come to symbolize love and affection, and they are highly recognized among the world's most popular commercially cut flowers. Their clove-like aroma, lengthy blooming season of about 8 weeks, and delicate, ruffled appearance have led to their stardom. Originally, the natural flower color of carnations was a pinkish-purple, but other colors have been developed over the years, including red, yellow, green, and white. Today, carnations are the national flowers of Slovenia, Spain, and Monaco; they are also the state flower of Ohio.

CLASSIFICATION

KINGDOM: *Plantae*

CLADE: *Tracheophytes*

CLADE: *Angiosperms*

CLADE: *Eudicots*

ORDER: *Caryophyllales*

FAMILY: *Caryophyllaceae*

GENUS: *Dianthus*

SPECIES: *D. caryophyllus*

BY THE NUMBERS

2	*common diameter size of flowers in inches*
31	*height of the plant in inches*
1907	*the year that the carnation was chosen as the emblem of Mother's Day*

COLLEGE CARNATION

Can carnations bring good luck? Evidently, students at Oxford University think so. According to tradition, students wear carnations to all of their exams. White carnations are for their first exam, progressing to pink and then red carnations for the final exam.

STICKY SOLUTION

When you touch a petunia, you might notice a sticky substance. Don't be concerned! The gooey sap that emits from the stems is ordinary and helpful. It is believed to be a deterrent against harmful pests and insects.

36. PETUNIA

Originating in South America, petunias are one of the most popular flowering plants and are cultivated worldwide. Though they prefer a warm and mild climate, they can be grown indoors to last through the winter months. Its name, "petunia," comes from the Brazilian word "petun," which means tobacco. In fact, the two plants are related, as they come from the same plant family (along with potatoes and tomatoes). Blooms can be single or bicolored, with varieties such as pink, white, purple, red, and blue. The five-lobed petals can have a ruffled texture and reach up to 5 inches in diameter.

BY THE NUMBERS

1	lifespan in years (treated as annual plants)
35	the number of petunia species
5+	hours of sun needed per day

PICK YOUR PLEASURE

Petunias are divided into four distinct groups. Grandiflora is the most popular and produces large flowers, while the hedgiflora type spreads quickly over large areas. The third, multiflora, is smaller but produces hardy flowers in hot and wet seasons. Lastly, milliflora types produce the smallest petunias, measuring only 1 inch wide.

ABOUT THE AUTHOR

Christin is the author of several books for kids, including many in the Little Library of Natural History. She lives with her family in California, where she enjoys rollerblading, puzzles, and a good book.